BIBLE INSIGHTS: BIBLE BOOK STUDIES FOR YOUTH

DANIEL

Trust Me!

By Thomas J. Doyle

SAINT LOUIS

Editor: Thomas A. Nummela

Editorial assistant: Phoebe W. Wellman

We solicit your comments and suggestions concerning this material. Please write to Product Manager, Youth and Adult Bible Studies, Concordia Publishing House, 3558 S. Jefferson Avenue, St. Louis, MO 63118-3968.

1 2 3 4 5 6 7 8 9 10   03 02 01 00 99 98 97 96 95 94

Contents

Welcome to Bible Insights!

Welcome to the Bible Insights Series of Bible studies for youth! These materials are designed to provide study opportunities that explore selected books of the Bible in depth and apply them to the real-life issues young people face. Each book in this series has been carefully prepared to speak to the needs and concerns of youth, providing insight from God's Word. Each book consists of four sessions of study that can be used for weekly Bible study, individual study, or for a Bible study retreat or seminar.

This book is designed for the leader of the sessions. It provides all the information and instructions necessary for an effective Bible study. Each chapter concludes with several pages you can reproduce for the students in your group. Additional background information on the Bible book to be studied and some helpful information about small-group Bible studies are included in the Introduction.

May God bless your study by the Spirit's power, as you lead young people to greater insight about God's Word and the good things God desires to bring through it to their lives.

Introduction

About This Course

The book of Daniel is an autobiographical record of a Hebrew who as a young man was taken captive by an invading army and imprisoned with many others in a far distant country. Daniel and his friends—among whom were Shadrach, Meshach and, Abednego of furnace fame—found themselves in a culture alienated from their God, hostile to their piety, and eager to discredit—and even destroy—them because of their faith. In His grace, God provided guidance, protection, and deliverance for Daniel and his friends. Similarly God provides guidance, protection, and deliverance for young people today who find themselves at odds with an ungodly world.

Daniel: Trust Me! will encourage young people to stand firm in their faith in a contemporary world that does not support their Christian faith and values, but rather attacks them. Each session addresses one of the ways in which young people are challenged to ignore God and to turn instead to self-indulgence, false wisdom, and idolatry.

Course Objectives

By the power of the Holy Spirit, young people who study this course will be able to
1. identify attitudes and activities that threaten their spiritual health;
2. seek the wisdom that only God's Word can provide for direction in their lives;
3. resist pressure from society or peer groups that would lead them away from God and His will;
4. share and live out their faith as they witness to those around them.

Some Background on Daniel

Daniel writes while living in Babylon. Daniel and many others from Judah had been taken from their homeland by King Nebuchadnezzar and held captive for more than 70 years. Daniel records things that happened to him, and visions he received from God, during his captivity. Daniel's story does not reveal whether he was among those who returned to Judah after the Exile.

The first three sessions of this study cover parts of Daniel's story while he and the others with him were still "young men," probably in their teens. The fourth session, dealing with the lions' den, takes place much later in Daniel's life—almost 75 years after he was taken into captivity. In the face of all that he experienced in the pagan culture of Babylon, it is evident that Daniel, by God's grace and power, remained faithful to the one true God.

The first six chapters of Daniel are narrative. They describe events that God uses to establish and protect Daniel and his friends in their captivity. They show God revealing Himself and His power to the kings Daniel is forced to serve. All four of our studies are taken from these narrative chapters.

The last six chapters of Daniel record dreams and visions God gave Daniel for the strengthening of His people in captivity. They reveal the future historical events God would later bring about to return His people from their exile and to fulfill His promise of a Messiah, Jesus Christ, the Deliverer. These prophecies so accurately predicted future historical events that some interpreters claim they must have been written much later than the Bible words claim.

God was clearly at work in Daniel's life. The ways in which He guides, protects, and delivers Daniel foreshadow the guidance, protection, and deliverance God provides today through His Son Jesus Christ for all believers—including the young people you will teach.

Have Fun As You Learn

Teenagers have a genuine desire to deal with life's tough issues. As God's Spirit works through the Word, young people grow in faith and in their lives of discipleship. These things will happen as young people study *Daniel: Trust Me!*

Today's youth also enjoy having fun. Strive early in the course to establish a casual, relaxed style. Teens live in a dynamic and fast-paced world. Plan your class in 10- to 15-minute blocks of time. Have optional or additional activities ready for groups or individuals who finish the task ahead of time. Be prepared to intervene when group discussion is "almost done" or side-tracked and move on.

Especially, evaluate the suggested activities for how they will work in your group, with your students and facilities. Adapt or replace activities that don't work with your group, so that the experience in its whole can be enjoyable and profitable for everyone.

Plan Ahead

With some advance planning you will be able to enhance the effectiveness of this course.

If your classroom does not have a chalkboard, you will need to purchase a pad of newsprint paper from an office supply or art-supply store.

Music is an important part of the life of teenagers. You might consider using one of the following as a theme song for the course: "Our God Is an Awesome God" by Rich Mullins (available in *The Group Songbook* from Group Publishing); "Soul's Celebration" by Terry K. Dittmer (available in *Singing Saints III*, produced by the Board for Youth Services, LCMS, 1333 S. Kirkwood, St. Louis, MO 63122; also on the cassette *Brothers and Sisters in Christ*, available from the same source or from Third Firkin below); or "Be Strong and Courageous" by Don Wharton (available on the cassette *Ready, Willing and Enabled* from Third Firkin Music Co., 23 Madison St., Suite 119, Madison, TN 37115, [615] 865-1890).

Building Relationships

The relationships between your students are a primary dynamic in any youth Bible class. These relationships are one of the primary reasons young people come together. They can be a tool you use to increase their enjoyment and their learning during the study sessions. Most sessions call for spending some time in small groups of three to five students. These small-group times allow individuals to express their faith, respond to challenging questions, and participate in a low-threat environment. They can be very productive times. Make the most of them.

Small Groups Are Key

Setting Up the Groups

If your class has more than five students on a regular basis, it is best to divide them into small groups. The ideal group size is from three to five students.

How the groups are formed is up to you. You can allow the participants to form their own groups. You could cluster students around birthdays (those born in January and February working together) or color of clothes (those wearing the most blue work together). Another fun way might be to have the students convert all numbers in their street address to a single number. For example, 292 North First Street becomes 2921. In a class of eight students, the four highest and the four lowest numbers would work together.

The Small-Group Advantage

Some might initially resist the idea of working in a small group. Working in small groups is often beneficial, since most people relate better in a small-group setting. In small groups,

• friendships are more easily established.

• the small number of persons lends to openness and willingness to share opinions and feelings.

• it takes less effort to integrate new people into small groups than into larger ones. Newcomers will feel more comfortable entering into a group of 4, as opposed to a group of 20.

The Empty Chair

Every small group should have one empty chair. That chair is available to newcomers. It will also encourage participants to invite friends to the group. Encourage students to invite unchurched friends to fill the empty chair.

You Are What You Eat

(Daniel 1)

Where We're Heading

"You are what you eat?" Though exiles and slaves, Daniel and his friends refused to eat the rich, royal foods intended for King Nebuchadnezzar's table, because they were not kosher (that is, they were not selected and prepared according Jewish religious regulations) and had been offered to idols. By God's grace, young people today can resist the idolatrous, ungodly choices offered by the world and often consumed by their peers.

Objectives

By the end of this session, participants will
1. identify things in their daily lives that are not "kosher" for Christians;
2. recognize the forces that pressure them;
3. rely on God to resist ungodly choices, and to know His forgiveness through faith in Jesus for times they fail.

Materials Needed

- Bibles
- One set of Student Pages 1–4 for each participant
- Pencils or pens
- blank paper for each participant
- Chalk and chalkboard or newsprint and markers (optional)

Bible Study Outline: You Are What You Eat

Activity	Minutes	Materials Needed
Warmup Activities	5	Scrap paper or chalkboard/ newsprint
We Choose	10	Student Page 1, pencils
Choices and Consequences	10	Student Page 2 pencils, newsprint or chalkboard
Daniel Chooses	15	Student Page 3, pencils, Bibles
Power to Make Good Choices	10	Student Page 4, pencils, Bibles
Closing Activity	5	Scrap paper, pencils, waste container

Warmup Activities

Choose one of the following activities.

Give each participant a piece of scrap paper. Ask participants to choose a food, food product, or menu item that best describes them and write it on the scrap paper. Some choices might include a Big Mac, Lean Cuisine, steak, or sandwich. Have volunteers name the food that best describes them and explain why.

Or . . .

Write "You are what you eat!" on the chalkboard or sheet of newsprint. Ask, "What does this saying mean to you?" Through the discussion that follows, help your students understand the philosophy that the things we consume affect us in substantive ways. Ask, "What are some examples of this philosophy?" High-cholesterol foods block arteries and cause heart disease, cigarette smoke causes lung disease and cancer, and alcohol damages brain cells and affects the nervous system.

We Choose

Distribute the Student Pages. Ask, "Do you ever eat a snack after school? If so, what are your favorite snacks?" Allow a few participants to respond, then direct everyone to the activity on Student Page 1. Instruct participants to select one food from every choice on the menu. After they have chosen foods from the menu, have them discuss the questions that follow in small groups.

When the small groups have had a few minutes to make and share their choices, invite reports to the whole class and then discuss the responses. Use the comments below to help direct this discussion.

1. Participants may choose a food because it tastes good, it's cheap, it's good for them, it's what their friends order, etc. Accept all reasons. (This is not primarily a nutrition class.)

2. While accepting all responses, watch for similarities in choices and reasons for those choices. Where such similarities occur, pose the question, "Why do you think your responses are so much alike?" Don't expect lots of answers; it is enough at this point to get them thinking about the question.

Choices and Consequences

Read aloud the opening paragraph. Pause after each question to allow volunteers to respond. Emphasize the fact that all choices have consequences. You may wish to write the words physical, emotional, intellectual, and spiritual on a chalkboard or a sheet of newsprint. Ask, "What might be some of the physical, intellectual, or even emotional or spiritual consequences of eating nutrious foods? junk foods?" Some possible responses are as follows:

Physical. Nutrition affects both our overall health and the energy we have.

10

Intellectual. Certain foods—or lack of food—can make us drowsy and inattentive, or hyperactive.

Emotional. In extreme cases, food choices may be the result of eating disorders that are psychological in nature. Guilt can be associated with some food choices. Other foods may bring good or bad memories.

Spiritual. Some religions prescribe or prohibit certain foods, at least at certain times. Eating or drinking things that we know have negative effects on our body or life could also have spiritual consequences in some cases.

After participants have had an opportunity to respond, have them complete the "Choices and Consequences" menu on Student Page 2 independently. When most participants have completed the activity, have them share in small groups their choices and the possible consequences of those choices.

Choices might include the clothes they wear, the friends they have; whether or not to be sexually active, to drink alcohol, to take drugs, to do their homework, etc. Consequences will vary. Challenge participants to decide whether or not the choices they make have physical, intellectual, emotional, and/or spiritual consequences. Point out that many choices we make have spiritual consequences. Remind participants that disobedience to God is sin and that "the wages of sin is death."

Daniel Chooses

Tell participants that Daniel and his friends had to choose whether to obey God or King Nebuchadnezzar. Whichever choice they made had possible deadly consequences.

Have participants work in their small groups to complete the choices section of the Bible study, Student Page 3. Give them 5–7 minutes to do so. Then review it with the whole group, inviting responses from groups or individuals. The correct responses are as follows:

Choice 1. Not to defile themselves with the royal food and wine.

Choice 2. Was afraid that the king would realize Daniel and his friends were not eating the royal food because they would look worse than the other men their age.

Choice 3. Looked better than the young men who ate the royal food.

Choice 4. Knowledge, understanding, and favor with the king.

After participants have completed the activity in small groups, point out that the royal food was offered to idols and unclean food that God had forbidden His people to eat. Discuss the questions that follow with the entire class. Use the following points to assist your discussion.

1. and 2. Undoubtedly, Daniel had to wrestle with the possible consequences of his disobedience to King Nebuchadnezzar—rejection, persecution, and possible death—and the consequences of his disobedience to God—separation from God and spiritual death.

3. Direct participants to complete the activity independently. Then allow volunteers to share their response and the reason for their response. Chances are, if honest, many participants would have to admit that they

would rather disobey God than face persecution and rejection at the hand of King Nebuchadnezzar.

Say, "Peer pressure, fear of rejection, and your desire to get ahead might have influenced your choice. Listen to St. Paul's experience." Read or have a volunteer read, **Rom. 7:21–25.**

Then say, "When we make the wrong choices we may say, 'What a wretched person I am!' We may ask, 'Who will rescue me from the body of death?' Fortunately, we may answer that question as did St. Paul, 'Thanks be to God—through Jesus Christ our Lord!' **(Rom. 7:25).** God sent Jesus into this world to suffer and die for all the times we make the wrong choices. By God's grace through faith we receive *complete* forgiveness of sins and the power to make choices in obedience to God.

Power to Make Good Choices

Tell participants, "God provides you the power to make choices in obedience to His will. The Holy Spirit works through these power sources (the means of grace) to strengthen your faith, so that you are able to make God-pleasing choices."

Read aloud the passages on Student Page 4. Have participants write the power source through which the Holy Spirit works on the line before each passage. The Holy Spirit works through God's Word, the Lord's Supper, Holy Baptism, and confession and absolution to strengthen our faith.

Tell participants that God provides these means to enable them to make wise choices. It is important that through regular use they are connected to these power sources—worship regularly, attend Bible study, attend the Lord's Supper, remember each day their Baptism, etc.

Closing Activity

Have participants list one or more of the choices they have made in disobedience to God's will on a piece of paper. Assure them that no one will see their responses. Pass a small waste can or other container around to each student. Have each participant crumple and hold up his or her scrap piece of paper, and say, "God, I am sorry for this and all my sins; forgive me." Each individual should tear up his or her scrap piece of paper, place it in the container, and pass it to the next person. When everyone (including you) has done this, read **1 John 1:8–9** (Student Page 4).

Conclude with a brief prayer of thanksgiving for the forgiveness of sins and the power of the Holy Spirit for making good choices in our lives.

(Your pastor could be invited to lead a brief service of confession and absolution incorporating this closing activity.)

We Choose

As you leave school, you decide to stop by the Snack Shop for a snack. Select one food from every choice on the menu.

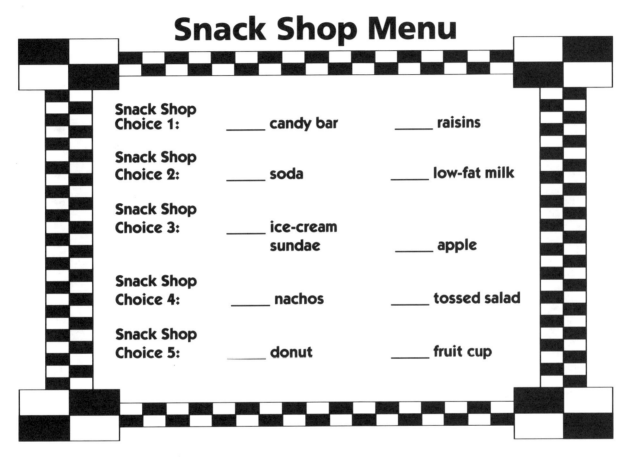

Snack Shop Menu

Snack Shop Choice 1: _____ candy bar   _____ raisins

Snack Shop Choice 2: _____ soda   _____ low-fat milk

Snack Shop Choice 3: _____ ice-cream sundae   _____ apple

Snack Shop Choice 4: _____ nachos   _____ tossed salad

Snack Shop Choice 5: _____ donut   _____ fruit cup

1. What was your reason for choosing each food?

2. Did most of your group make the same choices? For the same reasons?

Daniel, Student Page 1

Choices and Consequences

Often we must choose between what we know is good for us and what we like, but may not be good for us. Besides food, what other choices must we make? What factors influence those choices? All choices have consequences. What are some consequences of the choices we make? What are some physical, intellectual, emotional, or spiritual consequences of the choices we make? Complete the menu by listing choices you must make and the possible consequences of those choices.

Choices   Consequences

Daniel Chooses

Daniel and his Israelite friends had to make a choice. Use the menu below to help you focus on the choice Daniel was forced to make and the possible consequences of his choice.

Choose the best answer.

Choice 1. Daniel and his friends, as slaves to King Nebuchadnezzar, decided **(Daniel 1:8)**:

_____ to eat the royal food and drink the royal wine he offered rather than make the king angry and jeopardize their chances of earning a position in the king's court.

_____ not to defile themselves with the royal food and wine.

Choice 2. The king's official **(Daniel 1:9–10)**:

_____ immediately allowed Daniel and his friends to eat whatever they wanted.

_____ was afraid that the king would realize Daniel and his friends were not eating the royal food because they would look worse than the other men their age.

Choice 3. After 10 days Daniel and his friends **(Daniel 1:15–16)**:

_____ looked worse than the young men who ate the royal food.

_____ looked better than the young men who ate the royal food.

Choice 4. God gave Daniel and his three friends **(Daniel 1:17–20)**:

_____ knowledge, understanding, and favor with the king.

_____ persecution and rejection for choosing to disobey King Nebuchadnezzar.

© 1994 CPH **Daniel, Student Page 3A**

Daniel Chooses—Continued

1. What factors influenced the choices of Daniel and his friends?

2. What consequences might Daniel and his friends have had to face for their obedience to God and their disobedience to the king? What consequences would Daniel and his friends have had to face if they would have chosen to obey the king and disobey God?

3. On a scale of 1 (very unlikely) to 10 (very likely), how likely is it that you would have made the same decision as Daniel? Explain the reason for your answer.

Very Unlikely									Very Likely
1	2	3	4	5	6	7	8	9	1 0

Daniel, Student Page 3B   © 1994 CPH

Power to Make Good Choices

Through faith, God provided Daniel and his friends with the power to obey Him in spite of the possible consequences they might face for disobedience to King Nebuchadnezzar. God offers you the same power.

Read the Bible passages below to find out the means through which God provides you power to make God-pleasing choices. Write the power source on the line before each passage. The Holy Spirit works through these power sources to strengthen your faith, so that you can make choices in obedience to God.

God's Power Menu

_____ "Your Word is a lamp to my feet and a light for my path" **(Psalm 119:105)**.

_____ "This is My body, which is for you; do this in remembrance of Me" **(1 Corinthians 11:24)**. "This cup is the new covenant in My blood; do this, whenever you drink it, in remembrance of Me" **(1 Corinthians 11:25)**.

_____ "We were therefore buried with Him through baptism into death in order that, just as Christ was raised from the dead through the glory of the Father, we too may live a new life" **(Romans 6:4)**.

_____ "If we claim to be without sin, we deceive ourselves and the truth is not in us. If we confess our sins, He is faithful and just and will forgive us our sins and purify us from all unrighteousness" **(1 John 1:8–9)**.

2 What Do You Know?

(Daniel 2)

Where We're Heading

Daniel and his young friends exceeded their Babylonian counterparts in all wisdom and understanding **(Dan. 1:20).** They trusted "God in heaven who reveals mysteries" **(Dan. 2:28)** as they faced the demanding king who held their very lives in His hands. God continues to give wisdom, and especially makes us wise unto salvation.

Objectives

By the end of this session, participants will
1. describe the wisdom of Daniel and his friends, and its source;
2. know that all wisdom is not profitable or godly;
3. identify ways they can know God's wisdom;
4. rejoice in their knowledge of salvation and the other gifts God gives.

Materials Needed

• Bibles
• One set of Student Pages 5–7 for each participant
• Pencils or pens
• 10 index cards (optional)
• Chalk and chalkboard or newsprint and markers (optional)
• Various sources for finding answers to questions—telephone book, newspaper, magazine, encyclopedia, library book, radio, dictionary, Bible (optional)

Bible Study Outline: What Do You Know?

Activity	Minutes	Materials Needed
Warmup Activities	10–15	Index cards or several common sources of information
Answers to Questions	10	Student Page 5, pencils, newsprint or chalkboard
God's Answer for Daniel	15	Student Page 6, pencils, Bibles
God's Answer for Us	10	Student Page 7, pencils, Bibles
Closing Activities	10	drawing paper and markers, or lined paper and pencils or pens

Warmup Activities

Choose one of the following.

Find enough index cards for at least half the number of your participants. On the index cards write sources of answers to people's questions (e.g., newspaper, telephone directory, dictionary, encyclopedia, magazine, teacher, library book, radio, television, Bible.) Distribute the cards to volunteers in your class. Turn the class loose to play a game of "What am I?" Allow participants to ask the person holding an index card 20 yes or no questions. The goal is to figure out the source listed on the card. Do not tell participants at this time that each of the items listed on the index cards are a source for answers to questions. Remind participants that they can only ask questions that require a yes or no answer. After participants have guessed all of the items correctly, ask, "What do each of these items have in common?" If no one answers correctly, say, "Each of these items is a possible source for answers to questions."

Or . . .

Show the class the following items: a telephone book, a newspaper, a magazine, an encyclopedia, a library book, a radio, a dictionary, and a Bible. Ask, "What do all of these items have in common?" Write participants' responses on the chalkboard or a sheet of newsprint. Accept all answers. After the class has had an opportunity to brainstorm say, "Each item provides answers to questions. They are sources of information." Then ask, "What kinds of questions could each of these sources of information answer?" Accept all reasonable responses.

Answers to Questions

Distribute Student Pages 5–7 to each of the participants. Then read aloud the opening paragraph of Student Page 5. Allow participants to work independently or in small groups to list possible sources for answers to the questions. Some possible responses might include the following:

1. Newspaper, television advertisement, telephoning different stores
2. Friends, a telephone book, a newspaper ad
3. A newspaper, radio, television
4. A bakery, a cake mix box, a recipe book
5. The grades listed on returned tests and quizzes, the teacher
6. A dog breeder, a pet store, an encyclopedia, a library book about dogs
7. A friend, a neighbor, a newspaper, a sign in a store window
8. Television, newspaper, or magazine ads, cereal boxes
9. A library book about trees, an encyclopedia, a teacher, your own eyes
10. The Bible, a pastor or teacher, or anyone who knows the Bible

Allow participants to share their responses with the entire class. You may wish to list possible sources on the chalkboard or on sheets of newsprint. Then have a volunteer read the paragraph that follows the activity. Either in small groups or as a class, rank the reliability of some of the sources. Answers will vary. Point out to participants that advertisements sometimes provide misleading or inaccurate information.

Read aloud the final paragraph of this section. This paragraph connects the activity the participants just completed with the portion of Daniel they will study today.

God's Answer for Daniel

Read the directions for this activity aloud. You may need to give an example, since this activity may be difficult for some participants. Invite participants to complete this activity in small groups. Possible questions are as follows:

1. What was bothering King Nebuchadnezzar? Why couldn't King Nebuchadnezzar sleep?

2. What did King Nebuchadnezzar's wise men say to the king?

3. What did King Nebuchadnezzar threaten to do to his wise men, if they did not tell him his dream and interpret it?

4. How did the wise men respond to Nebuchadnezzar's demand?

5. What did King Nebuchadnezzar decree in response to his wise men's inability to interpret his dream?

6. What did God reveal to Daniel? How did God reveal Nebuchadnezzar's dream to Daniel?

7. How did Daniel respond to God's revelation?

8. To whom did Daniel give credit for his ability to know and interpret Nebuchadnezzar's dream?

9. What did Nebuchadnezzar's dream mean? You may wish to point out to participants that this portion of the dream predicts the coming kingdom of God that Jesus would usher in.

The first three kingdoms are those of Babylonia, Medo-Persia, and Greece. The fourth kingdom is the Roman Empire, into which Christ was born. Jesus is the rock that smashes the kingdoms of this world **(Daniel 2:44–45)**.

10. How did Nebuchadnezzar respond to Daniel's God-given ability to know and to interpret his dream?

Ask, "What do we learn about God from Daniel 2?" Accept all responses. Then say, "Only God can reveal to us true wisdom and knowledge in life-and-death matters. Today, God reveals His answers to difficult questions in His Word."

God's Answers for Us

Read aloud the opening paragraph. Then have participants work in small groups to write questions that each Bible passage answers. When each group has finished writing questions, have each share its questions with the entire class. Possible questions are as follows:

1. Who is sinful? Have I always been sinful?

2. What will happen to me because of sin? What is the result of sin?

3. What does God provide to repentant sinners? What will God do when we confess our sins to Him?

4. What did Jesus do for sinners? How much does God love us?

5. What do we know about Scripture? What does God's love for us in Christ equip us to do?

Read or have a volunteer read aloud the closing paragraph. Emphasize the reliability of God's Word as the source of information concerning life-and-death issues. Assure the participants of God's forgiveness through Jesus when we doubt, ignore, or look to other sources for information concerning these questions.

Closing Activities

Choose one of the following activities.

Have participants write a contemporary advertisement for God's Word as the only reliable source for answering difficult, or life-and-death questions. Allow participants to create an advertisement for television, radio, a newspaper, or a magazine. Allow time for participants to share their advertisements with the entire class.

Or . . . .

Have participants work in small groups to create a contemporary psalm praising God for their knowledge of salvation revealed in Scripture. Share the psalms as a closing worship activity.

Answers to Questions

Every day we obtain information from a variety of sources. What are some of the sources to which we turn for answers? To what source(s) would you turn in order to answer the following questions? List the source(s) after each question.

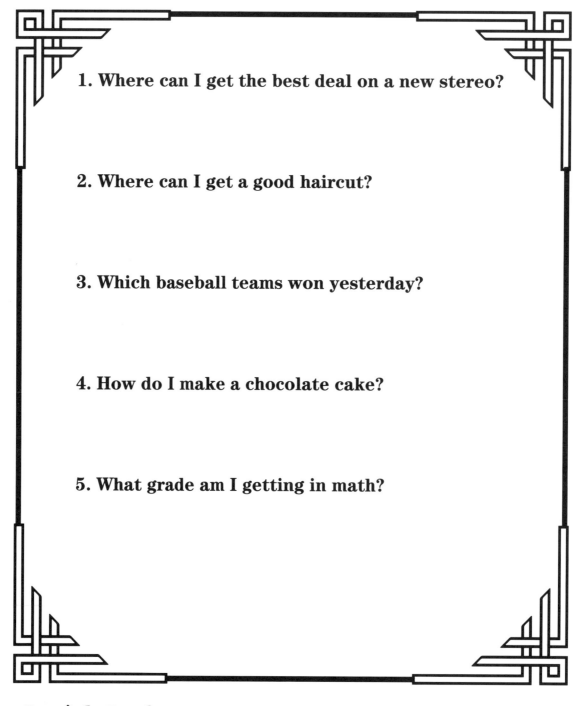

1. Where can I get the best deal on a new stereo?

2. Where can I get a good haircut?

3. Which baseball teams won yesterday?

4. How do I make a chocolate cake?

5. What grade am I getting in math?

Answers to Questions—Continued

6. What breed of dog makes a good house pet?

7. Where can I find a job?

8. Which breakfast cereal has the highest nutritional value?

9. Which trees lose their leaves in autumn?

10. How can I get to heaven?

Chances are that you can find answers to most questions from more than one source. **CAUTION:** Some sources are more reliable (likely to be true and accurate) than others. For those questions above that have more than one possible source for an answer, rank the reliability of each source beginning with 1 as most reliable, 2 as next most reliable, etc.

King Nebuchadnezzar asked Daniel a difficult, if not impossible, question. If unable to answer accurately the King's question Daniel and his friends faced a vicious decree, "I will have you cut into pieces and your houses turned into piles of rubble." Daniel turned to the only completely reliable source of information—God.

Daniel, Student Page 5B

God Reveals to Daniel an Answer to a Difficult Question

Read each of the following statements from Daniel 2. Write a question that each statement answers.

1. *In the second year of his reign, Nebuchadnez-zar had dreams; his mind was troubled and he could not sleep* (**2:1**).

2. *"O king, live forever! Tell your servants the dream, and we will interpret it"* (**2:4**).

3. *"If you do not tell me what my dream was and interpret it, I will have you cut into pieces and your houses turned into piles of rubble"* (**2:5**).

4. *"There is not a man on earth who can do what the king asks! . . . What the king asks is too difficult"* (**2:10, 11**).

5. *This made the king so angry and furious that he ordered the execution of all the wise men of Babylon* (**2:12**).

6. *During the night the mystery was revealed to Daniel in a vision* **(2:19a)**.

7. *Then Daniel praised the God of heaven* **(2:19b)**.

8. *"No wise man, enchanter, magician or diviner can explain to the king the mystery he has asked about, but there is a God in heaven who reveals mysteries"* **(2:27–28)**.

9. *"In the time of those kings, the God of heaven will set up a kingdom that will never be destroyed, nor will it be left to another people. It will crush all those kingdoms and bring them to an end, but it will itself endure forever"* **(2:44)**.

10. *"Surely your God is the God of gods and the Lord of kings and a revealer of mysteries, for you were able to reveal this mystery"* **(2:47)**.

God Reveals to Us Answers to Difficult Questions

God answers difficult questions about life and death issues in His Word. Read each of the following Bible passages and then write at least one question the passage answers.

1. Question(s):

God's answer: *Surely I was sinful at birth, sinful from the time my mother conceived me* (**Psalm 51:5**).

2. Question(s):

God's answer: *For the wages of sin is death . . .* (**Romans 6:23a**).

3. Question(s):

God's answer: *If we confess our sins, He is faithful and just and will forgive us our sins and purify us from all unrighteousness* (**1 John 1:9**).

4. Question(s):

God's answer: *You see, at just the right time, when we were still powerless, Christ died for the ungodly. Very rarely will anyone die for a righteousness man, though for a good man someone might possibly dare to die. But God demonstrates His own love for us in this: While we were still sinners, Christ died for us* (Romans 5:6–8).

5. Question(s):

God's answer: *And how from infancy you have known the holy Scriptures, that are able to make you wise for salvation through faith in Christ Jesus. All Scripture is God-breathed and is useful for teaching, rebuking, correcting, and training in righteousness, so that the man of God may be thoroughly equipped for every good work* (**2 Timothy 3:15–17**).

God's Word is always reliable. Often, because of sin, we may turn to less-reliable sources for information concerning difficult, life-and-death questions. Satan may tempt us to doubt the reliability of the information God provides to us in His Word. God sent His only Son into this world to live a perfect life and then to receive the punishment we deserved because of our sin by His death on a cross. God's love for us in Christ empowers us to trust in Him as we face all of life's challenging and threatening situations—including those with the most severe consequences.

3

What Would You Do?
(Daniel 3)

Where We're heading

Worshiping the god of gold in the face of the ultimate "peer pressure" could have been an easy choice for Daniel's friends; facing death they were confident of God's ability, though not certain of His intention, to save them from the king's wrath. Many young people, when they confirm their faith, make the vow to "suffer all, even death" rather then turn away from God. Through Christ Jesus, young people today are empowered to resist the idolatry of our age.

Objectives

By the end of the session, the participants will
1. identify the idolatry into which they are tempted by Satan, the sinful world, and their own sinful nature;
2. affirm that Jesus died for all sins, including their sins of idolatry;
3. express reliance upon Christ's strength to resist temptations of all kinds;
4. confess their faith in Jesus as number one in their lives.

Materials Needed

- One set of Student Pages 8–11 for each participant
- Bibles
- Pens or pencils
- 3" x 8 1/2" strips of white paper for making bumper stickers (These could be from white contact paper or other adhesive material.)
- Crayons, markers, and/or colored pencils
- Assortment of popular bumper stickers (optional)
- Newsprint and markers or chalk and a chalkboard
- Scrap sheets of paper (optional)
- A name tag for each participant, with the name of a thing that people might make into an idol (optional)

Bible Study Outline: What Would You Do?

Activity	Minutes	Materials Needed
Warmup Activities	10	Scrap paper and pencils or adhesive names tags
Bumper Stickers Tell the Story	10	Student Page 8, pencils, Bibles
Bumper Stickers Tell the Story of Shadrach, Meshach, and Abednego	15	Student Page 9, pencils, Bibles
What about Me?	10	Student Page 10, pencils, Bibles
A Bumper Sticker Tells the Story of God's Love for You	10	Student Page 11, pencils or markers;blank white strips of paper or white contact paper (optional)
Closing Activities	5	Bumper stickers students have made

Warmup Activities

Choose one of the following activities.

Play Make Me Laugh. Ask for a volunteer who believes he or she can make a participant laugh in one minute. Choose a participant for the subject of the test. Record the amount of time it takes for the volunteer to make the participant laugh. If the participant does not laugh after one minute, ask for another volunteer to try to make the participant laugh. After letting a number of participants play the game say, "We usually consider a person who laughs as a happy person. What makes a person happy?" List participants' responses on a sheet of newsprint or the chalkboard.

Or . . .

Give each participant a scrap piece of paper. Say, " 'Happiness Is' is the title of a song from the play *You're a Good Man Charlie Brown*. In this song each of the characters listed the things that made him or her happy. If you were to write the lyrics to the song, what things would you list?" Have participants work independently or in small groups to create a list of things they would include in the song. Then allow time for individuals to share their lists with the entire class.

Or . . .

Play What's My Idol? Explain that an idol is anything that people consider more important than God. Place a name tag on each participants' back. Say, "Each of you has the name of something on his or her back that people might consider more important than God. Ask questions of your classmates to try to figure out the item listed on your back." Use the following things as possible idols: grades, television, music, girl/boy friend,

29

clothes, being accepted by your friends, alcohol, sex, money, a car. When most or all participants have guessed the item written on the name tag on their back ask, "How might these items become idols? Can you think of other idols?"

Bumper Stickers Tell the Story

Distribute Student Pages 8–11 to each participant. Read aloud the opening paragraph of Student Page 8. Allow participants to discuss the attitude and priority promoted on the bumper sticker at the top of the page. The bumper sticker promotes "me-ism," happiness in acquiring things, and a disregard for a relationship with God.

Have participants then rank the list of things from 1 (most important) to 10 (least important) to determine their own priorities. Allow time for volunteers to share their ranking of the items with the entire class. Ask, "What does our ranking of these items tell us about our priorities?"

In the space provided, have participants use markers, crayons, or colored pencils to create a personalized bumper sticker that reflects the number 1 priority in their lives. Ask for volunteers to share their bumper stickers.

Now read, or have a volunteer read, **Ex. 20:3–4.** Invite participants to react to the Bible passage. Then say, "You may ask, 'What does that have to do with me? I haven't created or worshiped an idol.' Chances are you have broken the First Commandment again and again and again. For anything that takes higher priority in your life than God is an idol. Today, you will meet three men whose story is told in Daniel 3. These men were forced under great pressure to assess their priorities."

Bumper Stickers Tell the Story of Shadrach Meshach, and Abednego

Have participants work in small groups to complete the Bible-study activity on Student Page 9. Give each group markers, crayons, or colored pencils and at least six 3" x 8 1/2" strips of white paper. Urge groups to be creative when designing their bumper stickers to describe the events in the story. After most groups have completed their bumper stickers, allow time for groups to share their bumper stickers with the rest of the class. The information included on each group's bumper stickers will vary. The following brief description of each portion of Daniel 3 will help you measure participants' understanding of what they have read.

Dan. 3:1–3—King Nebuchadnezzar made a golden image.

Dan. 3:4–7—Nebuchadnezzar ordered all people to fall down and worship the golden image as soon as they heard the sound of music. Anyone who failed to worship the golden image would be thrown immediately into a blazing furnace.

Dan. 3:8–12—Some astrologers told King Nebuchadnezzar that Shadrach, Meshach, and Abednego refused to worship the golden image.

Dan. 3:13–18—King Nebuchadnezzar ordered Shadrach, Meshach, and Abednego to worship the golden image when they heard the music or face death in the blazing furnace. The three men refused to do as the king ordered. Instead, they confessed their faith in God to King Nebuchadnezzar.

Dan. 3:19–25—True to his word, Nebuchadnezzar had Shadrach, Meshach, and Abednego thrown into the blazing furnace because of their disobedience. The three men were not harmed by the fire. Instead, King Nebuchadnezzar observed them walking around with a fourth man, who looked "like a son of the gods." Many interpreters believe this fourth person was Jesus Christ, who stands with God's people in suffering and temptation. (Similar preincarnate appearances are found in **Genesis 18,** and **Joshua 5:13–15.**)

Dan. 3:26–30—The king praises the God of Shadrach, Meshach, and Abednego.

Discuss the questions on the Student Page with the entire class. Use the comments that follow in your discussion.

1. Chances are, if participants are honest, they would choose to worship the idol rather than die. We often worship idols even when we are not threatened.

2. Shadrach, Meshach, and Abednego probably felt frightened by the possibility of death, but confident that God would be with them whether they lived or died.

3. Most people would have the tendency to make Shadrach, Meshach, and Abednego the heroes of this story. God is the real hero in this story. For it was only through the faith God had given to Shadrach, Meshach, and Abednego that they were able to withstand the threat of death.

What about Me?

Most participants by this time will be aware of the fact that all people, including themselves, make idols. Discuss with participants the statements made by the high school students on Student Page 10. Have participants identify the idol each student may have made for himself/herself.

• Jack may have a dependency on alcohol. Anytime we depend on something God has created, rather than God, we have made an idol.

• Vicky has made her boyfriend an idol. She is willing to do anything to keep him, including breaking God's sixth commandment.

• Suzanne will do anything to be accepted, even stealing. Clothes and her desire to be accepted by her peers have become her idols.

• Mark's first priority is having fun, not God.

Urge participants to write about an idol they have made or their friends have made. Allow time for volunteers to share information about their idols or their friends' idols. **Caution:** Do not force participants to share if they don't want to.

Then say, "Jesus suffered and died on the cross for the times you 'make for yourself an idol.' God in Christ has paid the penalty for idolatry and all other sins. St. Paul proclaims the forgiveness Jesus earned for us on the cross in **Rom. 3:22–24.**" Read, or ask a volunteer to read, the passage aloud. Then ask for a student volunteer to tell in their own words what the passage says. Emphasize God's complete forgiveness through Jesus Christ for all sins, including idolatry.

Then say, "God's love for Shadrach, Meshach, and Abednego enabled them to make God number 1 in their lives, even when it meant possible death. God's love for you in Jesus will enable you to make God number 1 in your life. As your faith in Jesus is strengthened by the Holy Spirit working through God's Word, God will enable you to 'confess that Jesus Christ is Lord' and put Him first in your life."

A Bumper Sticker Tells the Story of God's Love for You

Have participants use markers, crayons, or colored pencils to create a bumper sticker in the space provided on the Student Page. Ask them to design a bumper sticker that tells of God's love for them in Jesus, God's power to enable them to resist temptations in their lives, or how God is number 1 in their lives. After participants have completed their bumper stickers, have them share them with the class as a possible closing activity.

Closing Activities

If participants created bumper stickers, have them share them with the class at this time.

Then pray a prayer like this one. "Dear God, give us strength through the power of the Holy Spirit so that we can resist the temptation to make idols in our lives. Help us instead to put You first always. We ask this in the name of Your Son, Jesus Christ, through whom we have forgiveness for all our sin. Amen."

Bumper Stickers Tell the Story

Bumper stickers often reflect the attitudes and priorities of people in our society. What attitude and priority does the following bumper sticker promote?

> ## THE ONE WHO DIES
> ## WITH THE MOST TOYS WINS!

Think about your priorities. Rank the following list of things from 1 (most important in your life) to 10 (least important in your life).

_____ Being accepted by your friends

_____ Having nice clothes

_____ Getting good grades in school

_____ Playing sports

_____ Learning a musical instrument

_____ Looking attractive

_____ Having a personal relationship with Jesus

_____ Working to earn money to purchase a car

_____ Having fun

_____ Telling your friends about Jesus

Compare your ranking of the items with others in your class. How does their ranking compare with yours? Create your own personalized bumper sticker to reflect your number 1 priority in life.

Bumper Stickers Tell the Story of Shadrach, Meshach, and Abednego

Read each of the following sections from Daniel 3. Then create a bumper sticker for each section that describes the events in that section.

- 3:1–3

- 3:4–7

- 3:8–12

- 3:13–18

Bumper Stickers . . . Shadrach, Meshach, and Abednego—Continued

- **3:19–25**

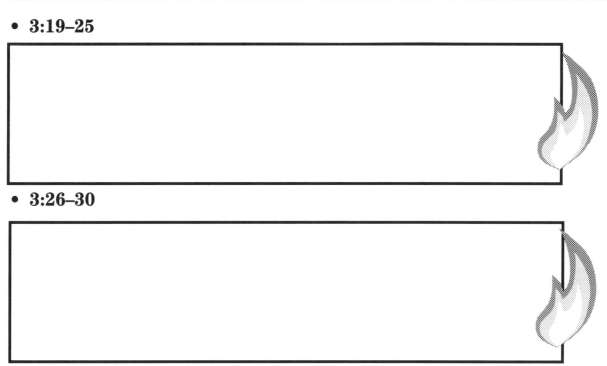

- **3:26–30**

When you have completed your bumper stickers, compare them with the bumper stickers other participants in your class created.

1. If you were given the choice, "Worship an idol or die," what would you do?

2. How do you think Shadrach, Meshach, and Abednego felt as they faced certain death in the fiery furnace?

3. Who is the hero in the story? (*Hint:* Reread the following bold confession of Shadrach, Meshach, and Abednego: "If we are thrown into the blazing furnace, the God we serve is able to save us from it, and He will rescue us from your hand, O king. But even if He does not, we want you to know, O king, that we will not serve your gods or worship the image of gold you have set up" **(Daniel 3:17–18).**

What about Me?

Satan, the world, and our own sinful self often will tempt us to make for ourselves "an idol in the form of anything in heaven above or on the earth beneath or in the waters below" **(Exodus 20:4).** Read the following statements by high school students and tell what idol they have made for themselves. Remember, anything or anyone that becomes more important to us than God is an idol.

Jack, age 16—"I just do it on the weekends. I mean . . . I have a lot of pressures during the week—grades, work, friends, a girl-friend. A couple of beers and I seem to forget all of my problems. Anyway, I'm not hurting anyone. Am I?"

Vicky, age 17—"I mean I really love him. If I don't give him what he wants, he's just going to find another girl who will. This is the '90s! I mean . . . everybody is doing it."

Suzanne, age 16— "My folks just can't afford to buy me the latest fashions. The store won't miss one or two outfits. If I don't wear the clothes my friends are wearing, I'll never fit in."

Mark, age 17—"Having fun—that's what life is all about. After a late night date, I'm too tired on Sunday morning to go to church or Bible study. Anyway, I'll have plenty of time for the 'church thing' after I'm out of high school."

Now it's your turn. Tell about an idol you or a friend has made. How has that thing or person become more important than God?

Name: _____, age:_____

"This righteousness from God comes through faith in Jesus Christ to all who believe. There is no difference, for all have sinned and fall short of the glory of God, and are justified freely by His grace through the redemption that came by Christ Jesus" **(Romans 3:22–24).**

A Bumper Sticker Tells the Story of God's Love for You

In the space design a bumper sticker that tells God's love for you in Jesus, the power God provides to you by the power of the Holy Spirit working through His Word, or how God is number 1 in your life. After you have completed your bumper sticker, show it to a friend and tell him or her about it.

What You're Up Against

(Daniel 6)

Where We're Heading

While living an upright life by God's grace, Daniel finds himself the target for envy and malice by the others of the present king's administration. In order to block his promotion, they engineer a law outlawing Daniel's worship of God. So too, God's young people today may expect not only temptation and pressure, but also active hostility as they witness their faith through their actions; only by God's power are they are enabled to face these forces with courage, confidence, and conviction.

Objectives

By the end of this session, participants will
1. share openly their concerns about living the Christian faith;
2. rejoice in their relationship with God and in the difference He has made in their lives;
3. rehearse possible responses to faith-related confrontations;
4. review God's ultimate victory through Christ on the cross.

Materials Needed

- One set of Student Pages 12–15 for each participant
- Bibles
- Pencils or pens
- Newsprint and markers or a chalkboard and chalk
- VCR and television and "The Hiding Place" video, available from most secular and Christian video dealers (optional)
- Newspapers and magazines (optional)
- Glue (optional)
- Scissors (optional)
- Large sheets of construction paper (optional)
- index cards (optional)

Bible Study Outline: What You're Up Against

Activity	Minutes	Materials Needed
Warmup Activities	10	Magazines and newspapers and large sheets of paper, markers, etc., or index cards
Facing the "Lions' Den"	10	Student Page 12, pencils
Daniel Faces a Lions' Den	15	Student Page 13, pencils, Bibles
Jesus Faces a "Lions' Den"	10	Student Page 14, pencils, Bibles
When You Face a "Lions' Den"	10	Student Page 15, pencils
Closing Activity	5	Video "The Hiding Place," TV and VCR (optional)

Warmup Activities

Choose one of the following.

Write the question, "What tempts you to disobey God?" on newsprint or the chalkboard. As participants arrive have them cut from newspapers and magazines pictures and words describing things that tempt them to disobey God. Then have participants work independently or in small groups to create a collage of temptations. Glue the words and pictures they cut out on a sheet of construction paper. Have them write the following Bible passage, or portions of it, on the collage: "Your enemy the devil prowls around like a roaring lion looking for someone to devour" **(1 Peter 5:8).** Have participants share their collages with the entire class.

Or . . .

Write on index cards temptations that high school students face (e.g., drugs, alcohol, cheating, stealing, going along with the crowd). Give volunteers a chance to pantomime the temptations listed on the cards. Have the class try to guess the temptation.

Facing the "Lions' Den"

Distribute the Student Pages 12–15 to each participant. Read aloud each of the situations on Student Page 12. Have participants work in small groups or independently to determine what they would say or do in each situation. Or have participants roleplay the situations. Accept all responses.

After each situation has been thoroughly discussed, read the closing paragraph in this section. Ask, "What lions' den did the characters in each situation face? What are some lions' dens that you face?"

Daniel Faces a Lions' Den

Direct participants to read Daniel 6. Then have them work in small groups to answer the questions. Tell participants to pay special attention to the questions included in the boxes. After most groups have completed the questions, discuss them with the entire class. The following comments will assist your discussion.

1. The administrators and satraps were jealous of Daniel.

2. The administrators and satraps could find no basis for charges against Daniel.

3. The administrators and satraps tricked the king into decreeing that anyone who prayed to a god other than the king for 30 days should be thrown into the lions' den.

Most people would be angry with those who were jealous of Daniel. They might feel hurt, betrayed, and powerless.

4. Daniel went to his room, opened his window, and prayed.

5. The men went to the king and told him that Daniel had ignored his orders.

Answers will vary to the questions in the box. Many people might deny their faith in God or try to hide their faith.

6. He was greatly distressed and was determined to rescue Daniel.

7. According to the law of the Medes and Persians no decree or edict that the king issued could be changed.

8. The king couldn't eat or sleep and at dawn hurried to the lions' den.

9. Daniel gave credit for his safety to God.

10. The king responded by believing in God and confessing His faith in the living God to his entire kingdom.

Jesus promises to be with you and help you when you speak out in faith about controversial issues, face ridicule or rejection, or have to make a decision contrary to what may be popular. God can use you as a powerful witness. The Holy Spirit, working through your witness of faith, can change the hearts of unbelievers.

Jesus Faces a "Lions' Den"

Work together to summarize the events in the Bible passages. Then compare Daniel's story with the events in Jesus' life. Suggested responses are indicated below.

John 11:45–53: The Jewish leaders, jealous of Jesus' popularity, looked for some way to bring charges against Him.

Matthew 26:59–60: The Jewish leaders looked for false evidence against Jesus, so they could put Him to death. They could find no evidence, even though false witnesses came forward.

Matthew 27:17–18, 24–25: Although Pilate knew Jesus was innocent, he allowed his decision to be swayed by the people.

Luke 23:40–41: The thief on the cross testified to Jesus' innocence.

1. Jesus and Daniel were both accused unjustly, leaders were jealous of their popularity, and both faced death because of their unwillingness to deny their faith.

2. Daniel lived. Jesus died so that we might live.

3. Because of Daniel's faithfulness, Darius saw the power of Daniel's God and came to believe in Him. As we in a similar way observe God's actions through the life of Jesus Christ, we too are brought to faith.

Your Next "Lions' Den"

Review with participants the situations on the Student Page. Once again, ask, "What are some 'lions' dens' you have faced, or are facing, because of your faith in Jesus?" Allow time for participants to respond. You may wish to write their responses on a sheet of newsprint or on the chalkboard.

Read aloud the closing paragraphs. Then say, "Empowered by the Holy Spirit working through Word and Sacrament you are equipped to face courageously the 'lions' dens' you may encounter." Urge participants to roleplay the situations on the Student Page, or "lions' dens" they may be facing, as people whom God has empowered to witness boldly their faith.

Closing Activities

If you have been able to locate it, begin to show "The Hiding Place." This is the remarkable story of Corrie Ten Boom, a person who faced persecution and death because of her faith. Once you have introduced it to the class, offer to complete the viewing at another time during the week.

Conclude this session with a prayer. Ask God to give you and the participants the power to witness boldly your faith and to do His will, even when facing a den of lions.

Facing the "Lions' Den"

What would you say or do in each of the following situations?

1. The waitress has just served your family the main course of the meal. Your father says, "Let's give thanks to God for this food." As you begin to bow your head you notice a group of the most popular kids in your school watching you and your family.

2. A couple of friends invite you to go on a Sunday outing to a popular amusement park. You have never been to this park and have always wanted to go. Although the park remains open late on Sunday nights, your friends, none of whom attend church, insist on leaving early in the morning. In order to go with them you will have to miss worship and Bible study.

Facing the "Lions' Den"—Continued

3. Your social studies class has discussed abortion. You realize from what students have said, that the majority favor a person's right to choose. Although he has never stated his position, it is obvious that the teacher also favors legalized abortion. You have learned from studying God's Word that abortion is a sin against the Fifth Commandment. You have even helped to distribute pro-life literature for the right-to-life group at church on Life Sunday. Five minutes before the end of the class the teacher says, "From our discussion today, it seems that no one in this class opposes abortion. Is there anyone in the class opposed to legalized abortion?"

Throughout history, people who believe in God have faced rejection, persecution, suffering, and even death for remaining faithful to God and His Word. These threats are often referred to as "facing a lions' den." Often we must face the threat of a "lions' den" because of our faith in God. Today, we learn how God enabled Daniel to remain faithful to Him, in spite of the threat of a gruesome death in the den of hungry lions.

Daniel Faces a Lions' Den

1. Why did the administrators and satraps try to find grounds for charges against Daniel? (See **Daniel 6:1–4.**)

2. What basis for charges could the administrators and satraps find against Daniel **(Daniel 6:5)**?

3. What plan did the administrators and satraps devise in order to get Daniel into trouble **(Daniel 6:6–9)**?

If you were Daniel, how would you feel toward the administrators and satraps?

4. How did Daniel respond to the king's decree **(Daniel 6:10–11)**?

5. What did these men do when they found Daniel praying **(Daniel 6:12–13)**?

Have you ever had the opportunity to demonstrate your faith, even when by doing so, you might offend someone, create an argument, or face ridicule? If so, what were the circumstances and how did you respond?

What would you have done if you knew that by demonstrating your faith in God you would face death?

Daniel, Student Page 13A

6. How did the king respond when he realized the administrators and satraps had tricked him **(Daniel 6:14)?**

7. Why was the king unable to reverse his sentence **(Daniel 6:15)?**

8. What behaviors of the king indicate that throwing Daniel in the lions' den troubled him **(Daniel 6:17–20)?**

9. To whom does Daniel give credit for his safety **(Daniel 6:21–23)?**

10. Because of Daniel's powerful witness of faith, in spite of terrible odds, how does the king respond **(Daniel 6:25–27)?**

**What promise does God provide to comfort, strengthen,
and encourage you when you speak out in faith about controversial
issues, face ridicule or rejection, or have to make decisions contrary
to what may be popular (Matthew 28:20b)?**

**How can God use you when you share His Word,
in spite of its seeming unpopular message?**

Jesus Faces a "Lions' Den"

Summarize the events in the following passages. Then compare Daniel's story with Jesus'.

John 11:45–53

Matthew 26:59–60

Matthew 27:17–18, 24–25

Luke 23:40–41

1. What similarities do you find between the story of Daniel and Jesus?

2. What was the result of Daniel's faithfulness? Jesus' faithfulness
(2 Corinthians 5:21)?

3. Because of Daniel's faithfulness,

Because of Jesus' faithfulness,

(See **Acts 2:23–24, 38; Romans 5:8; Romans 6:23b.**)

When You Face a "Lions' Den"

Review the situation on the first page of this lesson. What are some "lions' dens" you have faced or are facing because of your faith in Jesus? Did you or will you enter the lions' den? Or did you or will you avoid the lions' den by choosing that which is contrary to God's will?

Sometimes you will be tempted to avoid the lions' den by choosing to disobey God and His will. At these times you can turn to Jesus, confident that He died on the cross to forgive this sin and all others. His love for you will enable you to face new "lions' dens." Remember Jesus' final words to His disciples, "But you will receive power when the Holy Spirit comes on you; and you will be My witnesses in Jerusalem, and in all Judea and Samaria, and to the ends of the earth" **(Acts 1:8).** The Holy Spirit, working through Word and Sacrament, will enable you to witness boldly your faith in Christ, even when you face a "lions' den."

Write a prayer. . .

Daniel, Student Page 15